GRAHAM & FRIEDRICH, LLC
51 PROSPECT PLACE
BROOKLYN, NY 11217

Juan **Uslé** | ojo-nido

22 May – 5 July 2008

Juan **Uslé** | ojo-nido

Paintings and poems by **Juan Uslé**
With an essay by **Kevin Power**

L | A | LOUVER |

Juan Uslé: Beauty and All That Jazz

*In the world of saying and telling in which I first came into words, there is
a primary trouble, a panic that can still come upon me where the word no
longer protects, transforming the threat of an overwhelming knowledge into
the power of an imagined reality, or abstracting from a shaking experience
terms for rationalization, but exposes me the more. I seek in Poetry to go as
deep into "the passionate and fitful temper," as Plato calls it, of the soul
as the sense of relations and ratios can carry me.*

Robert Duncan — *The Truth and Life of Myth* [1]

I tend to suspect that shapes always come from somewhere known,
consciously or unconsciously, out of an image bank; perhaps they have to if
they are to feel alive, existing beyond the given formulas of aesthetics. In
Juan Uslé's work, these forms come through his eyes, or through the memory
lens of his camera, or through the accumulated telling of the history of his
own work. It is a matter of sight and insight. Zukofsky wrote years ago in *The
Objectivist Manifesto*, "Bring the lens up close." [2] The North American poet
was calling for a consuming clarity to see through, as it were, to the truth,
whereas in Uslé's case, it may well be a vital search to give rise to sensation, to
sharpen tension, and to stage a certain ambiguity that intrigues. He is con-
scious that truth cannot be unearthed, and that layers always cling beneath

---

[1]   Robert Duncan. *The Truth and Life of Myth: An Essay
      in Essential Autobiography.* Fremont, Mich.: The Sumac Press, 1968.
[2]   Louis Zukofsky; Charles Bernstein, fwd.; Mark Scroggins, ed. *Prepositions +:
      The Collected Critical Essays.* Middletown, Conn.: Wesleyan University Press, 2001.

appearance. We have intimations of recognition, of a definition, and of a final resolution, but perhaps, above all, we are engaging a suggestive force, a manifest energy, and a seduction.

Thus Uslé creates a space of subtleties and multiple satisfactions. Should we seek to know his values, his scales of measure, or the way in which he registers above-ground and underground activities—if those are the correct terms—for what are finally his flickering and fleeting sources, then I'd suggest the light through a window, down the valley in the morning, on his Saro stream, through the blinds of his Broadway flat, or the inexhaustible stimuli of snapping photos from his seat on a plane or on a subway, or moving through a tunnel under the Thames or in Rotterdam. Yet beyond this, make no mistake—Uslé's world is avowedly poetic: the mist amongst the chestnuts; black bread, white jug, red wine, goat cheese and a bunch of parsley on a table; pale green light through sunflowers; wasps and cobwebs in a barn; the white trunks of birches and their late autumn leaves on recently fallen snow; and light, however it chooses to manifest itself—sunlight solid and paralysed on the moon; light that is pure and empty and increases the etching of the shadows; chopped silver light at the river estuary; light seen as flakes of colour. I am, of course, proposing images, and Juan knows the list is inexhaustible, and as such constitutes an immense sense of relief. It separates his work from most of the abstraction we have around us, articulated through other parameters, more urban, more mental, and less adamantly and meticulously painterly.

Uslé is not a sharp kid on the block, but a complexly layered *pasiego* from Cantabria (an equally cool cookie who does not miss a beat), less given to the game but with all the acquired convolutions of perversity that thirty years of living in New York provide! He looks intently and weighs everything (sometimes twice). There is little urban nervousness, as if acutely aware, as Sartre reminds us, that we should not confuse nervousness with life, and it is life, thank god, that lies at the centre of his work.

Uslé's works are intense, whatever their scale, and they accumulate their own set of experiences: plays of colour, pressure of hands, dimension of brushstroke, size number of brush. They are records of a process that searches to become— and becomes—a presence. They are strangely calculated, avid of strangeness, and more complex than they initially seem. They accumulate as a series of layers that weave and mesh. And for those of us who know Uslé personally, they are much like the ramifications of his mind: an anarchic grid or a turbulent circular movement!

Uslé produces art, not cultural goods nor cultural commodities. It is a simple fact, but it distinguishes him from many artists of his generation. His work brings into play, as sole protagonist, our aesthetic judgement, and we have learnt to discern between something that desires the name of art and something that directly shelters under the umbrella of art. Aesthetic judgements are, should what I am about to affirm not simply be a Eurocentric bias, the conflation of the singular and the universal. Such judgement has the authority to propose a language that a priori lends value, even if unable on occasion to give such potential value a final and definitive shape. Painting is often stillborn, repetitive, afraid, or simply too often mediocre and miserably greedy. At its best, painting offers the experience of pleasure repeated. Uslé's best work renews our experience. Art may well now be a category of cultural commodities, but this is not what Uslé proposes—he looks at subjective experience through the privileged language of painting. I think it may well have been Wittgenstein who said that the last bastion of truth lies in language,[3] and language for Uslé—the language of painting—is the protagonist. He explores the dramas of syntax in what is both a metapictoric act and a closely woven commentary on his personal experience. He has a small world, yet, like Giorgio Morandi, it is also an immensity. Across his life he has worked with his landscape, his daily experiences, their rhythms and intensities, and now perhaps, above all, with the language through which he has expressed and experienced them. Uslé's work comes from and out of the paint. It emerges from what is happening, inclusive of accident, caprice, intuition and all slight tremors of sensibility, but at the same time, it is thought, as we say, thought through and through. The work looks back and holds our gaze and often stares us out.

There is a subtle and vibrant musicality to these works, uncomplicatedly and adamantly "romantic" as I have written on numerous occasions (although I wish, later in this essay, to introduce the qualification of "baroque"). He both knows and feels. His large series of black paintings, *Soñe que revelaba* (2004-08), is like Schubert's *Winter Journey,* nostalgic, muted, yet soaring, troubling, and satisfying.[4] The small works often have the brilliance and dazzle of Rachmaninoff as caught in the cascades of sound heard when Martha Argerich

[3]   Ludwig Wittgenstein. *Tractatus Logico-Philosophicus.* New York: Routledge, 2001.
[4]   Franz Schubert. *Die Winterreise.* 1827.
[5]   Martha Argerich. *Concerto for Piano no. 3 in D, Opus 30,*
        by Sergei Rachmaninoff. Berlin Radio Symphony Orchestra, 1982.

is laying down the law.[5] His work is pushed by an inner music tuned to the measures of the man. The paintings merge from small perceptions that demand time, perceptions that are pondered—but pondered through feeling. These small works can be seen as concentrated fragments, takes or cinematic frames. They don't seek to say it all, but they do seek to give the partial shape. Uslé knows there is in art a primary redemption of the world that is a new world created in the world. This is the place in which the individual human spirit comes alive to its own creation. The mind and hand find themselves wandering in their natural pluralities, a kind of multiphasic unity. I suspect that Uslé looks for forms that allow the most various feelings within him to find their inclusive but tailored articulation, where sympathies and aversions mingle.

Uslé leaves us little in doubt as to the nature of his sources, not specific names, but rather, stances towards reality. He writes, "Inside me there is a whole zone illuminated by romantic characters, perhaps more commonly associated with or belonging to the 19th century, dreamers and travellers, especially some of the last travellers. Yet there is also a zone that is highly open to connections with reality. These two zones are juxtaposed and struggle to hide themselves from each other. To the first, I owe my southern disposition, the incessant out-pouring of images that leave me giddy; and to the second, my attraction to light and a sense of peace. And to both of them, my commitment to the search for understanding from whatever it is I have close at hand: the gradual moving forward from my routines, from what is a modest and silent practice; an empirical rapprochement—tangible and daily—to space, materials and process. I find myself feeling more and more comfortable every day with this new zone—one that emerges from a stained and mottled penumbra—because

I know that it is precisely here that the other two grow, and that it is here that both the purest and the most contaminated images will appear. I find myself reflected in this practice, almost blinded by it, freed from desire, and given over to the process itself."

Kant has also meditated upon some of the problems that seem to preoccupy Uslé.[6] The German philosopher talks of *sensus communis* not as common sense, but as a common sentiment. In other words, a faculty for having feelings in common: both a communality and a communicability of feeling. This is what lies at the base of Uslé's work, and it is also what most radically separates him from other contemporary artists where concept often tends to preempt or preclude emotion. Kant suggests that the world is full of the strewn and often painful evidences of human behaviour and, at the same time, of the human capacity to share feelings. Uslé knows however that there is no proof that we do, in fact, share feelings in the same way, but there is a shared supposition that we do.

Uslé's work may spring on the one hand from the tradition of European and American abstraction—though it would be difficult to say specifically from whom in such a lineage—and on the other hand, from his perceptions, and from what Charles Olson has called "occasions."[7] His work imputes pleasures to us all and that makes it exceptional, even more so in these times when the

[6]   Immanuel Kant. *Critique of the Power of Judgment*. Cambridge:
        Cambridge University Press, 2000.
[7]   Charles Olson. "Human Universe." *Selected Writings*.
        New York: New Directions Press, 1967.

whole idea of Kantian "beauty" seems under question. Uslé acknowledges, I believe, that we can and do agree by feeling, and that it serves as a pointer to the transcendental or to the probability of the same. He often talks of surface, of the odd man out, of something that rivets the attention, and of the minims of speech that serve as tonal keys within his own language: a broken line, a pulsation, acts of complicity with the knowns, the borrowed, and the self-quotes, all contribute to the making of the unknown.

There is a constant push and pull on mind and feeling. These are works that have whispers at their edges: *Desacuerdo* (2007) with its overpainted red and yellow on the grey band, the line falling away to the right, and the square set out of balance to the left where we begin our reading before collapsing into a white void; *Outsider* (2006) that reminds us in the upper section of Lichtenstein's grid or Polke's exploitation of a plastic bubble wrapper impression, and running beneath it a series of crazy lopsided squares that appear as if they have all been wired up, whilst the intensity of the work gathers disturbingly at the bottom like a sediment; or *Sin Desenlace* (2007), with its horizontal bands overwritten by pulsating circular movement, by whiplashes or ribbons of pink, that produce a busy nervous complexity. And in this show at L.A. Louver, one might mention as extending in these same directions *El Templo* (2007-2008), with its vertical brushstrokes of ice-cream colors caught between horizontal strips that become alive through the broken lines that snake across their borders; or *Ojo-nido* (2008), where the not quite semicircular blue bands, more or less defined by white lines are suddenly invaded by the thrust of grey and rose echoing shapes that push into it, the latter like a small light bulb that illuminates all; or *Sueño de Salomón, 1* (2008) with its horizontal bands charged with mixed activities and events, apart from the final monochromatic blue; or *Erizado* (2008) with its characteristic horizontal bands with a step down produced by a twist of the hand, floating incomplete in space beneath a black line that appears like a trolley bus cable; or other inversions and variations upon these themes. The titles serve, in all probability, as a very small aperture into a larger area, and might be seen as keyholes or ways of getting into the painting. Yet, all I have said in relation to these works is finally description – evident and hopefully accurate. But the fact remains that description, as Robert Creeley has told us, simply hangs loose and delays.[8] It helps explain a formal construction, the building with a tested vocabulary, but it does not take us into the work. That, we know, is a more mysterious process. Uslé's dialogue with his work is a proof of our potential to care, to be moved by the Heideggerian idea of care for the other as one of the fullest definitions of love. I sometimes think that Uslé is looking for his own blind spot, a kind of intuitive recognition that love is the point where systems end and where surrender is made to contingency. Uslé is always pushing into his own emotions and pleasures, his hedonistic drive, whereby he constantly falls in love with what surprises him.

These works accumulate layers of meaning and of activity, and are more complex than they appear. They come close to what Uslé himself wrote recently in a notebook: "We seek exclusively to contaminate, to transmit a little emotion. The work should be understood as a reply, or more correctly, as a substantial composite of liberated material, reorganized and sustained

---

8   Robert Creeley. *The Collected Essays of Robert Creeley.*
       Berkeley: University of California Press, 1989.

by a complex organogram of experiences, questions and thoughts." The way to react to a painting is not through understanding, but through opening our pores to feeling.

These paintings strike us as beautiful, and for the need to recognize the beautiful as not a process of interpretation, but something more mysterious. It cannot be described adequately. In short, beauty calls. But from where? I am not sure that I can answer such a question, but I am equally sure that I can recognize it when I see it.

The problem remains, however, of how exactly does one move from a description of a work (a strong affirmative claim in itself) to a universal judgement. It is certainly a long jump and maybe an impossible one. Yet Kant provides us with an effort to answer this very question. Nevertheless, across the years we have come to doubt his answer. Kant argues that the free play of the imagination and understanding is the same in all human beings. Yet, we now know it isn't. We have also learnt that painting is a question of codes and language options. Uslé uses a lexicon that has its history—both its own history and as a part of a larger history of abstraction—and we who know this history also know he is adding something, small maybe but definitive. Kant insists that in making this claim, that *this is beautiful,* there is an a priori assumption that the pleasure is assumed by all. Uslé's work does everything to assure this through the exploitation of diverse strategies—shifts in register, in rhythm, in complexity, in noise and silence, in mass and line, in superposition and ground, and in what Cézanne called "les petites sensations" that are finally much larger in their impact than the phrase itself suggests.

Kant concludes that if you don't see *this is beautiful,* you don't have taste. And that for sure is quite a presumptive statement! Uslé's seductions are not—how could they be?—absolute, but over the years they have been continuous, and he now occupies a place close to the frontier where the beautiful asserts itself as possible, as elegance, imaginative flight, and polished particular. I do believe the option matters when so much work is simply polished, effete and saleable. I can hear George Oppen asking us if there is a difference between an apple given and one that is for sale![9]

While it is clear that aesthetic judgement does not command universal assent (*pace* Kant), it does throw up the question of such a possibility, and Uslé's world can best be explored in these terms. The images inevitably clutch at a fragment of his own reality and experience. We can all remember how Kandinsky saw battle scenes in his early abstractions, and how Paul Tortelier told fairy stories whilst rehearsing the Bach cello suites! Beauty creates smaller societies no less important or serious because they are partial and where each member is assiduously orthodox. This is the area in which Uslé works: control, concentration, imagination, astute interpretation of distinct linguistic elements, and an orchestrated largesse. At the same time he is himself clearly intrigued by the beauty of this reduced but infinite universe. This may well be what leads him to say that, "Perhaps progress lies in our capacity to renew the questions, to question ourselves."

---

[9]   George Oppen; Michael Davidson, ed. *New Collected Poems.*
        New York: New Directions Press, 2002.

Perhaps too simply, beauty is a luxury that only some can afford; poverty has little time for it. Is beauty a determinant in human life? Well, for many of us who have the time, yes, and for others quite clearly not! I have already mentioned that I would also like to qualify Uslé's romanticism as being nuanced by the baroque. Baroque is artful elaboration, the subtle dissimulation of an original model and its sublimation in the interplay of idiomatic figures and passages. In other words, a tuned and tensed musicality that serves as a counterpart to a romantic predisposition, willing to risk calculated accident as a permission to gain access to something that the artist is always waiting for. Uslé subjects his work to a constant compositional and even, on occasion, almost practical elaboration which itself becomes the centre of artistic interest in the new composition. He exploits his encounters along the borders of different worlds. I am thinking of the elegiac sumptuousness, the chanted calls on life and death, on beginning and end, palpable perhaps in *Soñe que revelabas* or the similar tensions, like the cut faces of a precious stone, that are equally present in *Doble Abierto* (2007) or in *O tiempo* (2007) where everything is held suspended by a small rectangle that rests of top of the extreme right vertical. Julia Kristeva wrote in *Black Sun: Depression and Melancholia* that the baroque reveals the cornerstone of its structure in the ornamental: "Artifice, as sublime meaning for and on behalf of the underlying implicit non-being, replaces the ephemeral."[10] I thought immediately not only of Uslé's work but

---

[10]   Julia Kristeva. *Black Sun: Depression and Melancholia.*
        New York: Columbia Univeristy Press, 1989. p. 99.

also of his human moods and perceptions of the world, his grasping at something for a meaning that is not there, through art, and the melancholy that such a conjuring trick finally bestows upon him. Uslé works obsessively, from an anguished sense that there is little else to do and an overriding need to do it. It is not an easy struggle, and pain enters the work, sublimated perhaps, but present.

So what can we see as baroque in these paintings: the rhythmic variations, a lingering dissonance hovering between things, a rapid trill or an accidental note, the mordent insertion, or the acid bite. These are all ornaments that register tonal uncertainties, shades of potential discord that characterize Baroque music and are part of Uslé's sense of what is going on in the world—in painting, in society, in nature, and in his own life. In a sense, he cannot believe what has happened. He is thankful but not impressed. Whereas he was once uncertain as to how long it would last, he now knows that the void is only his own, in himself, of his own making, and a constant companion that has to be explored and pushed to its limits.

William Bronk wrote in his essay "Desire and Denial": "Desire is our door into the world. We see shapes there and want them and we go after them into the world. But desire is our door out again also when the shapes we saw leave our desires unsatisfied. What could we ever have wanted? More than a door to enter, the world offers us a prospect to peer into whose shapes suggest a reality, which they, themselves, are not. And reality is what we want—our own or any

---

11   William Bronk. *Vectors and Smoothable Curves.*
      San Francisco: North Point Press, 1983. p. 51.

other—and reality is shapeless and disparate. We live in reality without posses-
sion or occupation and the love of reality unpossessed transfigures us."[11] Uslé
would sign that, and his work frequently does! He presents us with a world
that is susceptible to a poetics of ambiguity, and where repetitive design,
sinuous line, floods and explosive burst of color, as well as an awareness of the
light and darkness of our lives, can enter the universe of dream.

Kevin Power

El calor de tus piernas trenzadas en las mias,
y el vacío.
De los ojos que ya no están.

The warmth of your legs enlaced in mine
and the emptiness
in your eyes no longer there

Ojo-nido

2008, vinyl, dispersion and dry pigment on canvas
24 x 18 in. (61 x 45.7 cm)

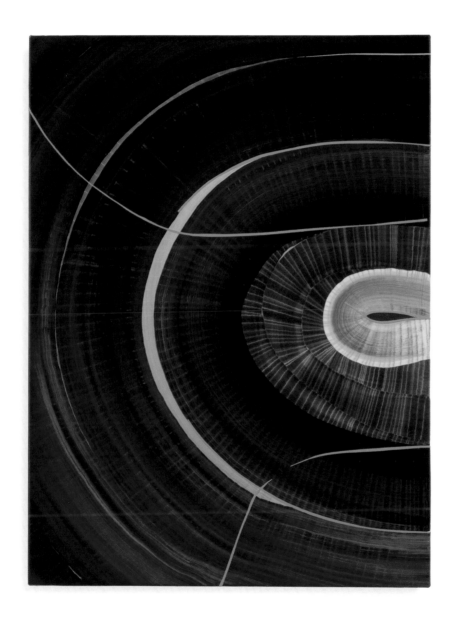

La luz está en tus ojos.
Y en tu mirada,
en esta noche oscura;
percibo aún las huellas de tus lágrimas.
Las de la historia,
las de la noche pasada.

The light in your eyes.
And in your glance,
on this dark night;
I can still see the traces of your tears.
Those of our story,
those from last night.

La Cámara Oculta

2008, vinyl, dispersion and dry pigment on canvas
18 x 12 in. (45.7 x 30.5 cm)

Busqué en vano tu palacio, y pregunté;
en vano a cada paso preguntaba.

I looked in vain for your palace, and I asked;
I asked in vain at every step.

Sueño De Salomón 2

2008, vinyl, dispersion and dry pigment on canvas
24 x 18 in. (61 x 45.7 cm)

Yo, cuando era estudiante, me debatía siempre
entre la necesidad imperativa de construir una bellísima torre de marfil,
y la necesidad, a la vez acuciante y placentera, de destruirla.

When I was a student I was torn
between the imperative necessity of building a beautiful ivory tower
and the need, both pressing and pleasurable, of destroying it.

Erizado

2008, vinyl, dispersion and dry pigment on canvas
24 x 18 in. (61 x 45.7 cm)

Ya te tengo, te dije, y te escapaste.
El amor es el silencio, me dijiste desde adentro.
La palabra destruye el amor y representa
solo a aquellos que son porque se nombran;
como el vacío, el desierto.

I've got you, I said, and you escaped.
Love is silence, you told me from inside.
Words destroy love and represent
only those who are because they can be named;
such as emptiness, the desert.

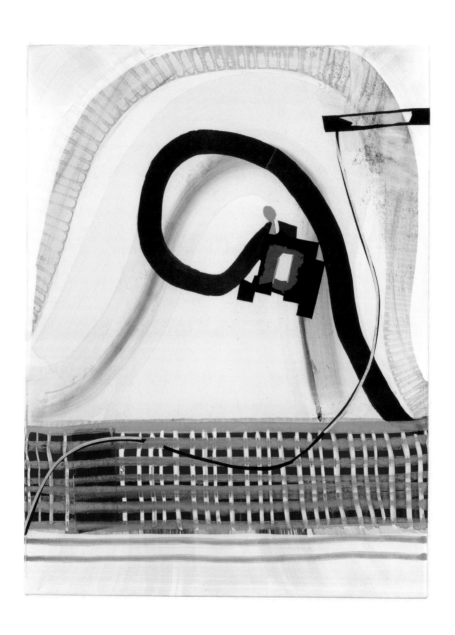

Mirando Hacía Afuera

2007 – 2008, vinyl, dispersion and dry pigment on canvas
24 x 18 in. (61 x 45.7 cm)

Solo pretendemos contagiar, trasmitir un poquito de emoción.
Las respuestas flotan descompuestas, sustanciadas de material liberado,
esperando reorganizarse de nuevo, con la mirada.
Todo sostenido por un complejo entramado,
de experiencias, preguntas y pensamientos.

We simply want to be infectious, to transmit a little emotion.
The answers float as bits and pieces, made up of freed material,
waiting to be reorganized again, through the eye.
All held together by a complex network of
questions, thoughts and experiences.

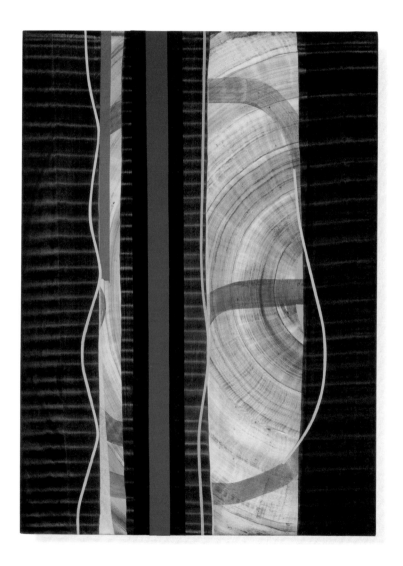

Nuevas Vidas

2008, vinyl, dispersion and dry pigment on canvas
22 x 16 in. (55.9 x 40.6 cm)

La imagen del tigre a contraluz,
camuflado, entre las tramas frescas de bambú,
esperando sigiloso el momento de saltar:
Al acecho.

Tiger caught against the light
camouflaged in the tight weft of young bamboo
silently waiting to assault
its prey.

The Warrior

2008, vinyl, dispersion and dry pigment on canvas
12 x 18 in. (30.5 x 45.7 cm)

En cada viaje me encuentro con un cuerpo,
que es cada vez más imagen de ti.
Cada vez más placer y más dolor cada vez,
más reflejo de ti, más olvido de mi.

On each trip I find a body
that is more and more an image of you.
Each time more pleasure and each time more pain,
a closer reflection of you, a fuller forgetting of myself.

Apretando Hacía Afuera

2008, vinyl, dispersion and dry pigment on canvas
22 x 16 in. (55.9 x 40.6 cm)

Tus ojos son el templo,
tu mirada el vacío.
Vuelvete a dormir hechicera.

Your eyes a temple
Your glance the void
Go back to sleep, spellbinder

Sueño De Salomón 1

2008, vinyl, dispersion and dry pigment on canvas
22 x 16 in. (55.9 x 40.6 cm)

¿Dónde escondes la brillante humedad de antaño:
entre archivos de memoria desatados ... o
en un rincón olvidado de tu estudio,
protejido por sueños desordenados?

Where are you hiding the damp brilliance of long ago:
amidst the scattered archives of memory ... or
in a forgotten corner of the studio
protected by disorganized dreams

Rocío

2007 – 2008, vinyl, dispersion and dry pigment on canvas
18 x 12 in. (45.7 x 30.5 cm)

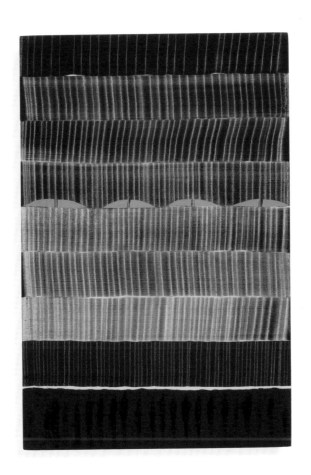

Cojiendote de nuevo me acomodo,
y en ti, casi entero duermo.
Afuera, los sonidos de Broadway,
los gritos, y las risas..., bien altos,
para hacernos confundir su estupidez
con otro material aún más absurdo:
el criminal murmullo de la guerra.

Taking hold of you again I make myself comfortable
and in you, I fall asleep almost completely.
Outside, the sounds of Broadway,
shouting and laughter ... very loud,
to make us confuse their stupidity
with something else even more absurd:
the criminal murmur of war.

Soñe que revelabas (Eufrates)

2008, vinyl, dispersion and dry pigment on canvas
108 x 80 in. (274.3 x 203.2 cm)

No pude contenerme y girándome les dispare de nuevo.
Vi que sus luces se "tornaban" despacio, tomando otro cuerpo,
ordenándose ahora en otra especie de estructuras mayores.
Un nuevo orden, desde fragmentos, unidades-partículas cuyas
siluetas recordaban formas casi reconocibles, como huevos,
galletas o tricotados. Ahora su voz no se escuchaba, pero
de nuevo, lentamente, mudaron sus formas.

I could not control myself and I turned round and opened fire again
I saw their lights spin slowly, taking another shape,
organizing themselves into another kind of larger structure
A new order, out of fragments, particle-units whose
outlines reminded us of almost recognizable forms, such as eggs
biscuits or knitting patterns. Now their voices could not be heard, but
once again, slowly, they changed their shape.

Los lumiacos

2008, vinyl, dispersion and dry pigment on canvas
18 x 24 in. (45.7 x 61 cm)

Te das la vuelta y lo ves,
te das de nuevo la vuelta y ya no lo ves.
Muchas veces, las paredes de tu estudio son como espejos,
donde se proyectan tus propias sombras y tus miedos.
Y por supuesto, mis propios deseos.

You turn round and see it
you turn round again and it's no longer there
the studio walls are often like mirrors
where your fears and shadows are projected
and, of course, my own desires

El Templo

2007 – 2008, vinyl, dispersion and dry pigment on canvas
24 x 18 in. (61 x 45.7 cm)

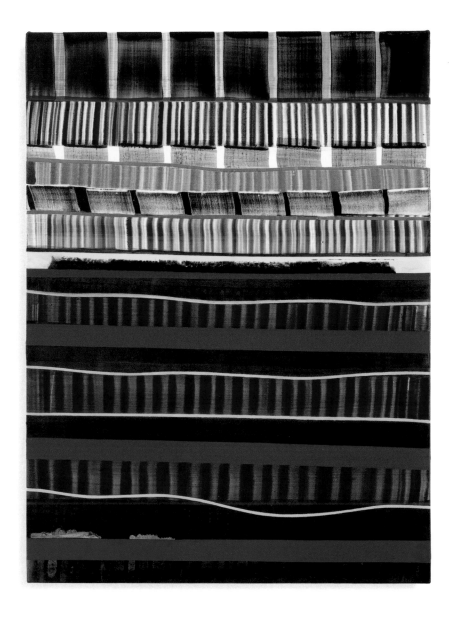

Comieron la cebada y les coloque cuidadosamente los auriculares.
Subí el volumen de aquella extraña música y los solte,
a pacer en aquella extensa pradera verde. Tan abierta,
justo detras de las alambradas de la zona norte.

They ate the barley and I carefully put the headphones on them.
I turned up the volume of that strange music and sent them out
to graze in the immense green meadow. So open,
just behind the barbed wire of the northern zone.

Overseas

2008, vinyl, dispersion and dry pigment on canvas
18 x 12 in. (45.7 x 30.5 cm)

Tus uñas escondidas en el campana río,
esperándome allí, tras la gran campana.
Traté de sujetarlas, desordenadas.
Pero se fueron rápidas, afiladas:
hacia la otra campana.

Your nails hidden in the bell tower
waiting for me, behind the large bell
I tried to keep hold of them, chaotic,
sharpened, they moved away too fast
to the other bell.

Good morning...

2008, vinyl, dispersion and dry pigment on canvas
16 x 22 in. (40.6 x 55.9 cm)

En animada conversación: el profesor, el pintor y el escritor, se sentaron a cenar.
Todo transcurría en armonía, hasta que los tres se empeñaron en explicar lo que veían
en el dibujo de las alas de aquella mariposa que, justo, acababa de posarse sobre la mesa.
La discusión creció, acalorada, hasta que apenas sin esfurzo aquel fragilísimo animal despareció.

In lively conversation a professor, painter and writer sit down to eat
Everything went well until the three of them started to explain what they saw
in the form of the wings of a butterfly that had just settled on the table.
The argument became heated until almost effortlessly the fragile creature disappeared.

Dropping Out

2008, vinyl, dispersion and dry pigment on canvas
22 x 16 in. (55.9 x 40.6 cm)

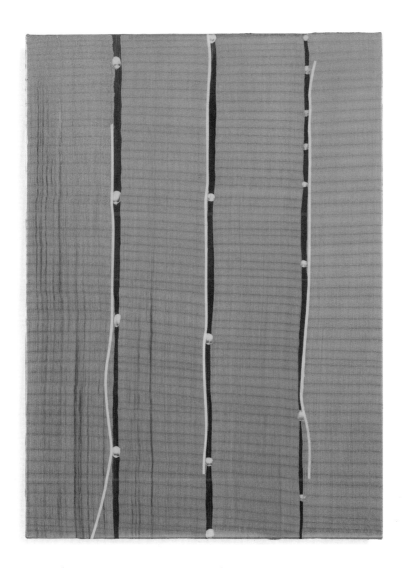

Si no logras descifrar su contenido
es porque te acercas a leer una pintura
como si se tratara de un acertijo.

If you can't make out its meaning
it's because you try and read a painting
in a glance, as if it were a cliché
as if it were a riddle

Escondido

2008, vinyl, dispersion and dry pigment on canvas
22 x 16 in. (55.9 x 40.6 cm)

JUAN USLÉ BIOGRAPHY

1954   Born in Santander, Spain
1973-77   Studied fine art at Escuela Superior de Belles Artes in San Carlos, Valencia

Lives and works between Saro (Cantabria) and New York City

SOLO EXHIBITIONS

2008   **Ojo-nido,** L.A. Louver, Venice, CA (5/22 – 7/5/08)
            Switch on / Switch off, Valencia Bancaja Headquarters, Valencia (4/1 – 6/30/08)
            Brezales, Cheim & Read, New York (2/7 – 3/15/08)

2007   **Switch on / Switch off,** Centro de Arte Contemporáneo de Málaga,
            Málaga, Spain (9/14-11/25/07)
            Galerie Thomas Schulte, Berlin
            Luz Aislada, Zoom, Santander, Spain

2006   Frith Street Gallery, London, England (3/3/06-4/21/06)
            En Otros Ojos, Galería Soledad Lorenzo, Madrid (6/22/06-7/15/06)
            Pieles y Miradas (with Victoria Civera), Galería Siboney, Santander, Spain

2005   **Alegre** (with Victoria Civera), Tim van Laere Gallery, Antwerp, Belgium, Belgium

2004   **Coágulo y Trama,** Galería Soledad Lorenzo, Madrid (6/24/06-7/24/06)
            Open Rooms, Fundación Marcelino Botín, Santander; SMAK,
            Stedlïjk Museum voor Actuale Kunst, Gante;
            IMMA, Irish Museum of Modern Art, Dublin

2003   **Open Rooms,** Palacio de Velaquez, Parque del Retiro, Madrid Spain (10/16/03 - 1/12/04)
            traveled to: S.M.A.K., Gent, April/May/June 2004, Fundacion Botin Santander
            Summer 2004; Imma Dublin September/October 2004
            New Painting, Galerie Thomas Schulte, Berlin, Germany

2002   Cheim & Read, New York
            Saro on paper, Van Laere Contemporary Art,
            Antwerp, Belgium, Belgium (12/5/02-1/18/03)
            Galerie Guislaine Houssenot, Paris
            First Time, Museum Morsbroich, Leverkusen, Germany

2001   **Llerana and Gramaland,** Galeria Joan Prats, Barcelona
            Quartos Escuro e Amarello, Museu Serralves/Museu de Arte Contemporanea,
            Porto, Portugal (5/18-7/8/01)
            Beauty & Sorrow, Galería Soledad Lorenzo, Madrid
            Llerana and Gramaland, Photographs, Galerie Thomas Schulte,
            Berlin, Germany (2/9 – 4/7/01)

2000   **Carmen del Negro,** Palacio de los Condes de Gabia,
            Diputacion Provincial de Granada Cultura: Area de Bienestar Social,
            Granada, Spain (5/5 – 6/25/00),
            traveled to Museo de Bellas Artes Ayuntamiento de Santander,
            Santander, Spain (7/7 – 9/2000)
            Noche Abierta, L.A. Louver Gallery, Venice, CA (5/23 – 7/1/00)

Distancia Insalvable, Museo de Bellas Artes de Santander,
Centro Cultural Caja de Cantabria, Sala Luz Norte;
traveled to Centro Cultural Casa del Cordon, Burgos, Spain
Palacete Embarcadero, Santander, Spain

1999   **Blind Entrance,** Cheim & Read, New York
Juan Uslé: Luz Aislada, Galería Estiarte, Madrid (June 1999)
Mantis, Galerie Buchmann, Cologne, Germany
La Mirada del Artista (with David Salle),
Galería Soledad Lorenzo, Madrid
644 Comun (with Victoria Civera), Van Laere Contemporary Art,
Antwerp, Belgium, Belgium

1998   **Recent Paintings,** Galerie Franck + Schulte, Berlin, Germany
Vanishing Lines, Galería Soledad Lorenzo, Madrid
With & Without Memory, Sala Robayera, Miengo, Spain

1997   **Luz Aislada,** Cheim & Read, New York
Everyday, Anders Tornberg Gallery, Lund, Sweden
Timothy Taylor Gallery, London, England
Galería Camargo Vilaça, Saõ Paulo, Brazil (with Victoria Civera)
Galerie Bob van Orsouw, Zurich, Switzerland

1996   **Back & Forth,** IVAM, (Instituto Valenciano de Arte Moderno), Valencia
Ojo Roto, MACBA, (Museo de Arte Contemporaneo), Barcelona
Ojo Roto, L.A. Louver, Los Angeles
Galerie Buchmann, Basel
1° de Mayo en Lund, Galería Soledad Lorenzo, Madrid

1995   **Lunada,** Robert Miller Gallery, New York
Sin Lugar - Singular, Galerie Buchmann, Cologne, Germany
Galerie Daniel Templon, Paris
Mal de Sol, Galería Soledad Lorenzo, Madrid

1994   **The Ice Jar,** John Good Gallery, New York
Frith Street Gallery, London, England (with Callum Innes)
Galerie Bob Van Orsow, Zurich, Germany
Namste, Palacio Provincial, Pontevedra
Peintures Celibitaires, Sala Amós Salvador, Logroño
Feigen Gallery, Chicago

1993   **Haz de Miradas,** Galería Soledad Lorenzo, Madrid
Figuraciones Tuyas, Anders Tornberg Gallery, Lund, Sweden
Peintures Celibataires, Galerie Barbara Farber, Amsterdam
1992   **Bisiesto,** Galería Joan Prats, Barecelona
Festina Lente, Sala de Exposiciones del Banco Zaragozano, Zaragoza
40 Ruby - 22 Riviera Blue, John Good Gallery, New York

1991   **Ultramar,** Palacete Embarcadero y Nave Sotoliva, Santander
Lado Prusia, Gallery Farideh Cadot, Paris
147 Broadway, Gallery Soledad Lorenzo, Madrid

1990   Gallery Barbara Farber, Amsterdam

1989   **Last Dreams of Captain Nemo,** Galería Montenegro, Madrid
Last Dreams of Captain Nemo, Galerie Farideh Cadot, Paris
Last Dreams of Captain Nemo, Farideh Cadot Gallery, New York

1988	Farideh Cadot Gallery, New York
	Gallery Fernando Silió, Santander
1987	Galería Montenegro, Madrid
	1960 Williamsburg, Galerie Farideh Cadot, Paris
1986	Galería La Maquina Española, Seville
	Palacete Embarcadero, Santander
1985	**Currents,** Institute of Contemporary Art, Boston
	Galería Montenegro, Madrid
	Gallery Windsor Kulturgintza, Bilbao
	Galerie 121, Antwerp, Belgium
1984	**Los trabajos y los dias,** Gallery Ciento, Barcelona
	Los trabajos y los dias. Las Tentaciones del pintor, Fundación Botín, Santander
	Los trabajos y los dias. Las tentaciones del pintor, Galería Nicanor Piñole, Gijon
1983	Galería Montenegro, Madrid
1982	Galería Palau, Valencia
1981	Museo Municipal de Bellas Artes de Santander
	Galería Ruiz Castillo, Madrid

GROUP EXHIBITIONS

2008	**Out of Storage 1.** Peintures choisies de la collection, MUDAM, Luvembourg
	Atemporalidad, Coleccion PECAR, Museo de Bellas Artes de Santander
	Espana 1957 – 2007. El Arte Espanol de Picasso a la Actualidad,
	Palazzo San Elia, Palermo
	Pasiones Privadas, Visiones Públicas, Marco, Museo de Arte Contemporánea de Vigo
2007	**Ver la Pintura,** Coleccion Coca Cola, Domus Artium, Salamanca
	Beijing Art Museum of the Imperial City, Beijing
	Pieles y Miradas (with Vicky Civera), Galería Siboney, Santander
	Nostalgia del futuro. Homenaje a Josep Renau, Museo de la Ciudad de Valencia
	Colección AINA de Arte Contemporáneo, Convento de Santa Inés, Seville
	Review, Galerie Thomas Schulte, Berlin
	Abstraction: extracting from the World, Millennium Galleries, Sheffield
	Visiones y expresiones. Colección de Arte Contemporáneo Fundación la Caixa,
	Fundación la Caixa, Barcelona
2006	**Hot Spring…in autumn,** Galerie Krisinger, Vienna
	Paradiso & Inferno, Galerie Academia Salzburg, Mario Mauroner Contemporary Art, Salzburg
	Nachaison / Alterseason, Hachmeister Galerie, Munster, Germany
	Floating Forms, Abstract Art Now, Wilhelm Hack Museum, Ludwigshafem am Rhein, Germany
	Colección 2006, CAAC, Seville
	El efecto Guerrero. Centro José Guerrero. Granada
	Last Call – Letzte Runde. Richard Deacon, Jonathan Lasker, Juan Uslé,
	Thomas Schulte Galerie, Berlin
	Tiempos de Libertad. Arte en España 1975 a 1990, Fundación Unicaja, Málaga
	Salvador Dalí and a century of Art from Spain, Salvador Dalí Museum, St. Petersburg, Florida;
	traveled to Alburquerque Museum, New Mexico
	Lucky Space. 15 ans de la collection d'art contemporain I.D.E.A, Mons, Belgium
	VIP III Arena der Abstraktion, Museum Morsbroich, Leverkusen, Germany

| 2005 | **Picasso to Plensa: A Century of Art from Spain,** |
| | The Albuquerque Museum, New Mexico 12/18/05-4/16/06 |

Picasso to Plensa: A Century of Art from Spain,
The Albuquerque Museum, New Mexico 12/18/05-4/16/06
The experience of Art, 51, Biennale di Venezia, Italian Pavilion, Venice
Yankee Love and Latin Doodle, Galerie Thomas Schulte, Berlin
Stromungen-Wasser in der Fotografie, Wacker & Jordanov, Munich
Colors-Stripes-Lines, Galerie Wolfgang Exner, Vienna
Hit you with a Flower, Tim van Laere Gallery, Antwerp
El Barco del Arte, Puerto de Bilbao
Sombra y Luz. Recorridos por el Arte Español, Instituto Cervantes,
Berlin, Brussels, New York, Rome, Vienna, Belgrade, Warsaw, Tel Aviv
Project Rooms, Arco 05, Madrid
Oronegro, Stand El Mundo, Arco 05, Madrid (with Victoria Civera)
Acentos en la Colección Caja Madrid. Pintura española contemporánea .
Sala de las Alhajas, Madrid
Hasta pulverizarse los ojos. BBVA Contemporáneos 2005. Madrid and Bilbao.
Tiempos de libertad. Arte en España 1975-1990. Caja España, León
Señas de identidad. Palacio Episcopal. Málaga
Experiencias. Museo de Bellas Artes de Santander
Febril la mirada. Galería Manuel Ojeda. Las Palmas de Gran Canaria
Fotografiá, Galería Estiarte, Madrid
Summer Eyes / Summarize 2005, Jan Weiner Gallery, Kansas Eyes

2004
Coagulo y Trama, Galería Soledad Lorenzo, Madrid
Rooms, Fundacion Marcelino Botin, Santander, Spain;
Irish Museum of Modern Art, Dublin, Ireland
Open Rooms, SMAK, Ghent, Belgium
Monocromos: De Malevich al presente,
Museo Nacional Centro de Arte Reina Sofía, Madrid
The Widening Gyre, Rubicon Gallery, Dublin
Nine Little Giants, Galerie Tomas Schulte, Berlin
On painting, Jan Weiner Gallery, Kansas City
Fragmentos: Arte del XX al XXI, Colección Pilar Citoler, Centro Cultural de la Villa, Madrid
Summer, Tim van Laere Gallery, Antwerp
Summer Eyes / Summarize 2004, Jan Weiner Gallery, Kansas Eyes
Contemporánea arte, Sala Amós Salvador, Logroño
Reubicación, Galería Xavier Fiol, Palma de Mallorca
Colección Testimonio 2003 – 2004, Fundación "la Caixa",
Sala de Exposiciones Plaza Conde de Rodezno, Pamplona

2003
New Abstract Painting – Painting Abstract Now,
Museum Morsbroich, Leverkusen, Germany
Distintas Miradas, Museo Municipal de Arte Contemporaneo de Madrid
Watercolor: In The Abstract traveling exhibition curated by Pamela Auchincloss
The Hyde Collection, Glens Falls, NY 9/30 - 12/09
Michael C. Rockefeller Arts Center Gallery SUNY at Fredonia 1/18/02 - 2/22/02
Butier Institute of American Art, Youngstown OH 3/10/02 - 4/28/02
Nina Freundenheim, Inc., Buffalo NY, May 11 - July 15 2002
Ben Shahn Gallery Williams Patterson University Wayne NJ 9/6/02 - 10/11/02
Sarah Moody Gallery of Art, University of Alabama, Tuscaloosa,
11/3/02 - 12/14/02 extended until 4/15/03
Before and after Science, Marella Arte Contemporanea, Milan, Italy
Abstraction in Photography, Von Lintel Gallery, New York
Memoria de un recorrido, Collección Caja de Burgos,
Circulo de Bellas Artes de Madrid, Italy
Collección Aena de Arte Contemporaneo, Museo de Bellas Artes, Santander
Rooms, Museo Nacional Centro de Arte Reina Sofia, Madrid
Don´t think twice, it´s all right, Van Laere Contemporary Art, Antwerp

Museo de Museos: 25 museos de Arte Contemporáneo en la España de la Constitución, Museo Nacional Centro de Arte Reina Sofía, Madrid
Simple Marks, Cheim & Read, New York.
Mano a mano: 25 años de construcción democrática, Centro Cultural de la Villa, Madrid
New Abstract painting - Painting Abstract Now, Museum Morsbroich, Leverkusen,
Distintas miradas, Museo Municipal de Arte Contemporáneo de Madrid

2002   **Summerdays,** Tin Van Laere Gallery, Antwerp
Zenroxy, Von Lintel Gallery, New York, (12/26/02 - 2/1/03)
Volume 1 Van Laere Contemporary Art, Antwerp, Belgium, (1/24-3/2/02)
Margins of Abstraction, Kouros Gallery, (7/10-9/7/02)
Galería Blancpain Stepczynsky, Geneva
Alma del norte, Mercado del Este, Cantabria
Abstracciones 1950 – 2000, Fundación Telefónica, Santiago de Chile
El Siglo de Picasso en las colecciones del MNCARS, National Gallery of Athens

2001   **Camera Works,** Marianne Boesky Gallery, New York, (6/28-8/10/01)
Liquid Properties, Cheim & Read, New York, (7/06/-8/20/01)
Content is a Glimpse, Timothy Taylor Gallery, London, England (11/07 – 12/21/01)
Concepts of images, New York based artists 2001, Gallery Academia
and Galerie Mario Mauroner, Salzburg
Col·lecció Testimoni 2001 – 2002, Centro de Arte La Regenta, Las Palmas de Gran Canaria
Colección Fundación Coca-Cola España, Sala Fundación Caja Vital KuTexasa
Colección Banco Zaragozano. Arte contemporáneo,
Sala Picassa del Círculo de Bellas Artes, Madrid
La Colección del Museo Nacional de Arte Reina Sofía, De Picasso a Barceló,
Museo Nacional de Buenos Aires
Encrucijada. Reflexiones en torno a la pintura actual,
Sala de Exposiciones de Plaza de España, Madrid
La noche, Imágenes de la noche en el arte español, 1981 – 2001,
Museo Esteban Vicente, Segovia
Drawings, Frith Street Gallery, London
Generación, Galería Moisés Pérez de Albéniz, Pamplona
Shap photographies, Baltimore Museum, Baltimore
Visiones del Paisaje, Polvorín de la Ciudadela, Pamplona
Colección De Pictura, Pintura Española 1950 – 2000, Museo de Bellas Artes, Santander
Arte español de los ochenta y noventa en las colecciones del MNCARS, MNCARS,
Museo Nacional Centro de Arte Reina Sofía, Madrid

2000   **Eurovision,** Saatchi Gallery, London, England (1/13 – 4/2 00)
Photographs by painters, photographers, sculptors,
Lennon, Weinberg Gallery, New York
Diálogos con la fotografía, Galería Soledad Lorenzo, Madrid
Flash Back (80,5), Barbara Farber / La Serre, Chateau Vallat, Trets-France
Super-Abstraction, The Box, Turin; traveled to Galerie Les Frilles du Calvaire, Paris
Painting Language, L.A. Louver, Los Angeles
Pintura Europea actual – Un encuentro entre el norte y el sur (Colección de
Tore A. Holm; traveled to Centro de Exposiciones y Congresos de Zaragoza
Colección de Arte Contemporáneo Fundación "la Caixa." Pasajes de la colección en
Málaga, Sala de Exposiciones del Palacio Episcopal de Málaga
Visiones de la Colección de Arte Contemporáneo de la Fundación "la Caixa,
Fundación "la Caixa", Palma de Mallorca
Reconstructions: The Imprint of Nature/The Impact of Science,
Sidney Mishkin Gallery, Baruch College, New York (2/4 – 3/2/00)
Universal Abstraction 2000, Jan Weiner Gallery, Kansas City, MO (1/7 – 2/29/00)
Opulent, Cheim & Read, New York, NY (6/14 – 9/1/00)

Lasker, Marcaccio, Uslé, Marcel Sitcoske Gallery, San Francisco, CA (9/16 – 10/28/00)
Small Work, Nina Freudenheim, Inc., Buffalo, NY (10/21-11/22/00)

1999 **Abstrakt:** Eine Definition abstracter Kunst an der Schwelle der neuen Milenium,
Max Gandolph Bibliothek & Galerie Thaddaeus Ropac, Salzburg
Art Lovers, Tracey, The Liverpool Biennial of Contemporary Art, Liverpool
Painting Language: Rotation in the development of the paintings,
LA Louver, Venice, CA (12/2/99 – 1/8/00)
Europa-Edition, Portfolio Kunst A.G. Neuen Austellungshalle, Vienna
El Salto del Caballo, Galería Lekune, Pamplona
Pintura Europea Actual: Colección Tore A. Holm, Palau de Pedralbes, Barcelona
Art per a Artistes, Centre d'Art Santa Mònica, Barcelona
Espacio pintado, Centro Cultural Conde Duque, Madrid
Photographic Works by Sculptors, Painters, Photographers,
Lennon, Weinberg, New York (12/11/99 – 1/22/00)
Free Coke, Greene Naftali Gallery, New York
Powder, Aspen Art Museum, Aspen, CO
Nollaig Shona, Green on Red Gallery, Dublin, Ireland
Together/Working, University of New Hampshire,
curated by Judith Swirsky (9/2/99-10/10/99)
Imágenes de la Abstracción, Sala de las Alajas, Madrid
La mirada del artista: Photografias, (Juan Uslé and David Salle)
Galería Soledad Lorenzo, Madrid
Reconciliations, curated by Jeffrey Hoffeld, DC Moore Gallery, New York (fall 1999)
Abstraction, Galerie Daniel Templon, Paris (10/30 – 11/30/99)
Photographic Works by Sculptors, Painters, Photographers,
Lennon, Weinberg Gallery, New York (12/1199 – 1/22/00)

1998 **Undercurrents and Overtones,** CCAC (California College
of Arts & Crafts), San Francisco, CA
Adquisitions, Museum Moderner Kunst Stiftung Ludwig, Viena
Arterias, Malmo Konshall, Malmo
The Body, Blind Spot Slide Show, Photographic Center of Skopelos, Greece
Small Paintings, Cheim & Read, New York, (7/1-7/31/98)
Exploiting the Abstract, Feigen Contemporary, New York (5/2-6/13/98)
EV + A 98, Limerick City Gallery of Art, Hunt Museum, Limerick, Ireland
Blind Spot, Issue 10, Soho Triad Fine Arts, New York (1/15/98 – 2/17/98)
Paisajes de un Siglo, Palacio Almundi, Murcia
Territorio Plural. 10 años Colección Testimonio, 1987-1997, Fundación La Caixa Madrid
Pinturas, Galería Siboney, Santander
Fabrica de deseos, 20 artistas españoles contemporáneos,
Galería Xavier Fiol, Palma de Mallorca
La Mirada Ecléctica. Colección Alberto Corral, Palacete del Embarcadero, Santander
Painting Language, L.A. Louver Gallery, Los Angeles (8/5-9/5/98)
Exposición Colección Testimonio, Edificio Pignatelli, Zaragoza

1997 **Theories of the Decorative: Abstraction & Ornament in Contemporary Painting,**
Royal Botanic Garden, Edinburgh, Scotland (8/9/97 – 10/5/97)
Traveled to: Edwin A. Ulrich Museum of Art, Wichita State University,
Wichita, Kansas (10/30/97 – 12/30/97)
Colecció d'Art Contemporani Fundació "la Caixa," Centre Cultural
de la Fundación "la Caixa", Paseo de San Juan, Barcelona
Abstraits, 4 Artistes au Quartier, Centre d'Art Contemporain de Quimper, France
Abstraction/Abstractions~Conditional Geometries (geometries provisoires),
Musée d'Art Moderne, Saint-Etienne
En la Piel de Toro, Palacio de Velázquez, Madrid
Arte Contemporáneo Español, Colección MNCARS, Palacio de Bellas Artes, Mexico DF

Colección Testimonio 96-97, Estación Maritima, La Coruña
FIA 97, Galería Camargo Vilaca, Caracas
Nuevas Abstracciones Españolas, Galería Manuel Ojeda,
Las Palmas de Gran Canaria
Procesos, Casa de Osambela, Lima
Arte Español para el Fin de Siglo, Sala de las Atarazanas,
Valencia and Tecla Sala, Barcelona
Pintura, Galería Joan Prats, Barcelona
Geometrias en suspensión, Palacio de la Merced, Diputación de Córdoba, Córdoba
Españoles de los 80, Sala de la Alhóndiga, Segovia

1996   **Theories of the Decorative,** Baumgartner Galleries, Washington, DC
Group Show, Robert Miller Gallery, New York
Nuevas Abstraciones, Palacio de Velazquez, Madrid
Abstrakte Malerei, Kunsthalle Bielefeld
Noves Abstracions, MACBA, Barcelona
Art at Work, Banque Bruxelles Lambert, Brussells
Natural Process, Lafayette College, Williams Center for the Arts,
Easton, Pennsylvania; Center Gallery, Bucknell University,
Lewisburg, Pennsylvania & Locks Gallery, Philadelphia
Transitions, Galerie Farideh Cadot, Paris
Group Show, L.A. Louver, Los Angeles
1985-1996. Obra origianal sobre papel, Colección Fundesco,
Sala de Exposiciones de Telefónica, Madrid
Arte Español para el Fin de Siglo, Centro Cultural Tecla Sala,
L'Hospitalet de Llobregat, Barcelona
John Chamberlain/Juan Uslé. Photographs in connection
with one sculpture/one painting, Galerie Buchmann, Cologne
Ecos de la Materia, MEIAC, Badajoz
Aquellos 80, Casas del Águila y la Parra, Consejeria de Cultura,
Santillana del Mar, Cantabria

1995   **The Adventure of Painting,** Würtembergischer Kunstverein, Stuttgart;
Kunstverein für die Rheinlande und Westfalen, Düsseldorf
Transatlantica: American-Europe Non representativa,
Museo de Artes Visuales Alejandro Otero, Caracas
Tres Parelles, Gallery Dels Àngels, Barcelona
Colección Testimoni 94-95, Fundación "la Caixa", Palma de Mallorca
A Painting Show, Galleri K, Oslo
New York Abstract, Contemporary Arts Center, New Orleans
L.A. International, Christopher Grimes Gallery, Santa Monica
Architecture of the Mind: Content in Contemporary Abstract Painting,
Galerie Barbara Farber, Amsterdam
Human-Nature, The New Museum of Contemporary Art, New York
Timeless Abstraction, Davis MacClain Gallery, Houston
On Paper, Todd Gallery, London
Embraceable you: Current Abstract Painting, Moody Gallery of Art,
University of Alabama, Tuscaloosa

1994   **Painting Language,** L.A. Louver, Los Angeles
Fall Group Exhibition, John Good Gallery, New York
Couples, Elga Wimmer Gallery, New York
A Painting Show, Deweer Art Gallery, Otegem, Belgium
Dear John, Sophia Ungers Gallery, Cologne
Mudanzas, Whitechapel Art Gallery, London
Possible Things, Bardamu Gallery, New York
Reveillon '94, Stux Gallery, New York

Watercolors, Nina Freudenheim Gallery, Buffalo
Works on Paper, John Good Gallery, New York
Artistas Españoles Años 80-90, Museo Nacional Centro de Arte Reina Sofia, Madrid
The Brushstroke and its Guises, New York Studio School of Drawing, Painting and Sculpture, New York
New York Paintings, L.A. Louver Gallery, Los Angeles
About Color, Charles Cowles Gallery, New York
Contemporary Abstract Paintings, Grant Gallery, Denver, CO
Embraceable you: Current Abstract Painting, Pritchard Art Gallery, University of Idaho;
Selbig Gallery, Ringling School of Art and Design, Sarasota and Moody Gallery
of Arts University of Alabama
Abstracción: a tradition of collecting in Miami, Center for the fine Arts, Miami
Testimonio Fin de Siglo, Diputación de Huesca, Huesca

1993   **Cámaras de Fricción,** Galeriá Luis Adelantado, Valencia
Desde la Pintura, Museo Rufino Tamayo, Mexico DF
Jours Tranquilles a Clichy, Paris & New York
XIII Salon de los 16, Santiago de Compostela; Palacio de Velázquez, Madrid
Malta's Cradle: Reflections of the Abyss of Time, Solo Impression Inc. New York
Obras Maestras de la Colección Banco de España, Museo de Bellas Artes, Santander
1973-1993, Dessins Americains et Européans, Galerie Farideh Cadot, Paris;
Baumgartner Galleries, Washington, D.C.
Testimoni 92-93, Sala Sant Jaume, "la Caixa", Barcelona
Verso Bisanzio, con Disincanto, Galleria Sergio Tossi, Arte Contemporaneo, Prato
Impulsos y Expresiones, Círculo Cultural de la Fundación "la Caixa", Granollers
Sueños Geométricos, Arteleku, San Sebastián; Galeriá Elba Benitez, Madrid
Single Frame, John Good Gallery, New York

1992   **Documenta IX,** Kassell
America Discovers Spain 1, The Spanish Institute, New York
Los 80 en la Colección Fundación "la Caixa", Antigua Estación de Córdoba, Seville
Pasajes, EXPO'92, Pabellón de España, Seville
23 Artistes pour l'annee 2000, Galerie Artcurial, Paris
Tropismes, Tecla Sala, Fundación "la Caixa", Barcelona
A look at Spain, Joan Prats Gallery, New York
Collecció Testimoni 91-92 "la Caixa", Barcelona
Production of Cultural Difference, III Istanbul Biennial; Spanish Institute, New York

1991   **Imágenes Líricas: New Spanish visions,** Sarah Campbell Gallery, University of Houston;
Henry Art Gallery, University of Washington, Seattle; The Queens Museum of Art, New York
Suspended Light, The Swiss Institute, New York
John Good Gallery, New York
Drawings, Pamela Auchincloss Gallery, New York
Col-lecció Testimonio 90-91, "la Caixa", Barcelona

1990   **Imágenes Líricas: New Spanish Visions,** Albright Knox Gallery, Buffalo, New York;
The Art Museum at Florida International University, Miami
Inconsolable: An exhibition about Painting, Louver Gallery, New York
Painting Alone, The Pace Gallery, New York
VIII Salon d'Art Contemporain de Bourg-en-Bresse
Abstract painter, L.A. Louver, Venice, CA

1989   **Época Nueva: Painting and Sculpture from Spain,** Meadows Museum,
Southern Methodist University of Dallas; Lowe Art Museum,
University of Miami, Coral Gables, Florida
Imágenes de la abstracción, Galeriá Fernando Alcolea, Barcelona
Primera Trienal de Dibujo Joan Miró, Foundació Miró, Barcelona
Crucero, Galeriá Magda Belotti, Algeciras

1988   **L'Observatoire,** Salle Meridiane, L'Observatoire, Paris; Farideh Cadot Gallery, New York
              Life, Death, Eternity, A.F.R. Fine Art, Washington
              España Oggi, Artisti Spagnoli Contemporanei,
              Rotonda di Via Besana e Studio Marconi, Milan
              L'art arrive de partout, B.A.C.-88 (Bienal de Arte Contemporaneo), Lorraine
              España, Mincher & Wilcox Gallery, San Francisco; Museo de Monterrey, CA
              Pintura de Vanguardia en Cantabria, Universidad de Santander
              Epoca Nueva: Painting and Sculpture from Spain, The Chicago Public Library,
              Cultural Center, Chicago; Akron Art Museum, Ohio

1987   **Pintura Española: La generación de los 80,** Museo de Bellas Artes de Alava;
              Santiago de Chile; Buenos Aires; Montevideo; Rio de Janeiro; Caracas; Mexico
              Les Bras de la Memoire, Galerie Christine la Chanjour, Niza
              Spanish Painting in New York: Two Eras, Baruch College Gallery, New York

1986   **Spanish Bilder,** Kunstverein, Frankfurt; Hamburg; Stuttgart
              1981-86: Pintores y Escultores Españoles, Fundacion Caja de Pensiones,
              Madrid; Fondation Cartier, Jouy-en-Josas, France
              Periferias, Centro Cultural de la Villa, Madrid
              Pintar con Papel, Circulo de Bellas Artes, Madrid
              Arte Español Actual, Palacio de la Moncloa, Madrid

1985   **XXIII Bienal de São Paulo,** Brasil
              Tercera Bienal Internacional de Dibujo, Nuremberg, Germany; Linz, Austria
              Cota ± Cero sobre el nivel del mar, Diputación Provincial de Alicante;
              Pabellón de Villanueva, Jardin Botanico, Madrid; Museo de Bellas Artes,
              Seville; Sala Parpalló, Valencia

1984   **En el Centro,** Centro Cultural de la Villa, Madrid
              IV Bienal Nacional de Arte de Oviedo, Museo de Bellas Artes, Oviedo
              Adquisiciones, Museo Español de Arte Contemporáneo, Madrid

1983   **26 Pintores, 13 Criticos: Panorama de la Joven Pintura Española,** Sala de Exposiciones
              de la Caja de Pensiones, Madrid; Museo de Arte Contemporaneo, Caceres;
              Museo Municipal de Bellas Artes, Santander
              Preliminar, Primera Bienal Nacional de las Artes Plásticas; Museo Provincial de Zaragoza;
              Museo Municipal de Bellas Artes de Santander; Palau Meca, Barcelona
              14 Pintores Cántabros Contemporáneos, Museo Municipal de Bellas Artes, Santander
              III Salón de los 16, Museo Español de Arte Contemporaneo, Madrid

MUSEUMS AND COLLECTIONS

Albright Knox Museum, Buffalo
Artium-Museo de Bellas Artes de Álava, Vitoria
Autoridad Portuaria, Santander
Birmingham Museum of Art, Birmingham, Alabama
CAC Málaga
Centro Atlántico de Arte Moderno, Las Palmas de Gran Canaria
Centro Andaluz de Arte Contemporáneo de Sevilla
Centre Pompidou, Musée National d'art Moderne, Paris
Collecció Testimoni, "la Caixa", Barcelona
Collection Norte, Gobierno de Cantabria
Arte Contemporáneo Fundación "la Caixa", Barcelona
Colby College Museum of Art, Waterville
Consejería de Cultura, Turismo y Deportes, Gobierno de Cantabria

Fonds National d'Art Contemporain, Ministère de Culture, Paris
Foundation AENA. Colección de Arte Contemporàneo
George Eastman House, Rochester
Guggenheim Museum, Bilbao
Herreriano, Valladolid
Irish Museum of Modern Art, Dublin
Instituto Valenciano de Arte Moderno, Valencia
MIGROS, Museum für Gegenwatskunst, Zurich
Moderna Museet, Stockholm
Musée d'Art Moderne, Luxemburg
Museo de Arte Contemporàneo Español, Patio
Museo de Bellas Artes de Santander
Mueso de Torrelaguna, Madrid
Museo Extremeño e Iberoamericano de Arte Español Contemporàneo, Badajoz
Museo Nacional Centro de Arte Reina Sofía, Madrid
Museu d'Art Contemporani, Barcelona
Museu Serralves, Porto
Museum Marugame Hirai, Japan
Museum Boijmans van Beuningen, Rotterdam
Museum Moderner Kunst Stiftung Ludwig, Vienna
New York Public Library, New York
Parlamento de Cantabria, Santander
Stedelijk Museum voor Actuele Kunst, Gante
Staatsgalerie Moderner Kunst, Munich
Staatsgalerie, Stuttgart
Städtisches Museum Schloß Morsbroich, Leverkusen
Tate Modern, London
University Art Museum, Long Beach, California
Zimmerli Art Museum, New Jersey

CREDITS

Library of Congress Control Number: 2008931331
ISBN 0-9765585-7-2

© 2008 L.A. Louver and Juan Uslé. All works by Juan Uslé
© Juan Uslé. All rights reserved. No part of the contents of this book
may be reproduced, in whole or in part, without permission
from the publisher L.A. Louver.

Juan Uslé portrait by Vicky Uslé Civera
L-R: Ruben Gonzalez, Victoria Civera, Juan Uslé
Artwork photography by Robert Wedemeyer
Translation by Kevin Power

Edited by Lisa Jann
Design by Stefan G. Bucher for 344design.com
Printing by Typecraft, Wood & Jones, Pasadena, California

L.A. Louver
45 North Venice Boulevard
Venice, CA 90291
Tel 310.822.4955
Fax 310.821.7529
www.lalouver.com

L | A LOUVER |

VENICE, CALIFORNIA
LALOUVER.COM